The
FRIENDLY
FOUR

Eloise Greenfield

Illustrations by Jan Spivey Gilchrist

 HarperCollins*Publishers*

Amistad

Library of Congress Cataloging-in-Publication Data
Greenfield, Eloise.   The friendly four / Eloise Greenfield ;
illustrations by Jan Spivey Gilchrist.— 1st ed.   p.   cm.
ISBN-10: 0-06-000759-1 (trade bdg.) — ISBN-13: 978-0-06-000759-1 (trade bdg.)
ISBN-10: 0-06-000760-5 (lib. bdg.) — ISBN-13: 978-0-06-000760-7 (lib. bdg.)
1. Friendship—Juvenile poetry. 2. Children's poetry, American.
3. Summer—Juvenile poetry. I. Gilchrist, Jan Spivey, ill. II. Title.
PS3557.R39416F75 2006   2005018588   811'.54—dc22

Typography by Carla Weise
1 2 3 4 5 6 7 8 9 10
❖
First Edition

CONTENTS

ONE

Drummond

Who I Am

Drum: I'm Drummond Anthony Liggins,

mostly known as Drum,

who likes to wrestle,

likes to run,

likes to count

things.

I count my footsteps

from the porch to the gate,

and I wait.

Wait for fun to find me

in my big back yard.

Bummer Summer

Drum: Not many kids live on my block,

two teens, two babies, and me.

Summer's a bummer,

nobody to chase,

nobody to catch the ball

I throw.

Hurry up, September!

Get here, fall!

so I can be with

all my friends again.

After the Baby

Drum: *I am bored!*

I've already talked to my baby brother,

played with my cars,

read two books with the babysitter,

worked a puzzle, and watched TV.

The babysitter said

she's going to take me

to the playground,

after the baby finishes his nap,

after the baby's diaper is changed,

after the baby eats,

after this, after that.

When Mama and Daddy get home

from work,

I'm going to make sure

they see me pout,

because "after the baby"

takes too long,

and I just want to go

out!

Neighbors

Drum: New family moving in down the street,

one man, two women, a parakeet.

But wait! I can't believe my eyes,

a girl who's just about my size.

What kind of neighbor would I be,

if I didn't go down and see?

Stand nearby and say hello,

I'm someone they'll want to know.

I can do it, I'm not shy,

all I have to do is try.

Well, maybe tomorrow, I'll be brave.

Today, I'll just sit here and wave.

TWO

Drum **and** Dorene

Meeting Dorene

Drum: Hi.

Dorene: Hi.

Drum: I came with my mother

          to say hello,

          I saw you yesterday.

Dorene: I know. I saw you, too.

Drum: Do you want to play outside?

          I have a yard that's long

          and wide, just right for running.

          Come on, I'll show you

          the way.

Dorene: Okay. Grandma, can I go out

          and play?

The Race

Drum: Let's run three times in a big circle.

Dorene: I'm jumping up and down. I'm ready.

Drum: Whoever touches this big tree first

         is the winner.

Dorene: I'm jumping up and down! I'm ready!

Drum: On your mark, get set, ready . . .

Dorene: I'm gone!

Drum: Come back! I didn't say, "Go."

Dorene: Just kidding. Hurry up, hurry up and

         say it.

Drum: Ready, go!

Drum and Dorene: Running fast around the yard,
breathing hard, we're track stars,
pushing our elbows back,
leaning around the turns, churning
our legs like bicycle wheels.

Dorene: Once around the track.

Drum: Twice around the track,
three times, I'm ahead!
I win! I slap the tree!

Dorene: Only a little ahead of me.

Drum and Dorene: Huffing, puffing! Whew!

Tall Tale

Dorene: You want to know where I lived before?

Drum: Uh-huh.

Dorene: Okay, well, I used to live in a place where it was easy to go up a hill, and hard to go down.

Drum: Yeah, sure.

Dorene: And in the winter, all the people would drag their sleds to the bottom of the hill, and then they would ride up.

Drum: Right.

Dorene: Well, one icy night, I slipped and fell, and I slid all the way to the top of the hill and hurt my leg, and the people tried to carry me down, but they all kept sliding back up.

Drum: Uh-huh, I really believe that.

Dorene: So we lived on top of the hill all winter, and as soon as the ice melted, we packed up our things and moved here.

Drum: Uh-huh, sure, right!

14

The New Boy

Dorene:	Ms. Lynn Bunton has a new son.
Drum and Dorene:	She said he is the perfect one,
	for her.
Drum:	We think he'll be perfect
	for us, too. He's six,
Dorene:	we're seven.
Drum and Dorene:	He's having a party
	today at eleven,
Dorene:	for Drum, himself and me.
Drum and Dorene:	We can't wait to meet him,
	then two friends will be three.

THREE

Drum, Dorene and Louis

Someone

Louis: My new mama really looks at me,

not at all like the other two,

who looked past me into nothing.

My new mama's eyes turn soft,

when she sees me,

like the eyes of someone

I think I knew,

once, a long time ago.

I wonder if it was

my mother.

The Party

Louis:	I'm glad you came. Do you want to play a game?
Drum and Dorene:	Okay.
Louis:	Spin the arrow, move the piece around the board.
Dorene:	Move it forward.
Drum:	Move it back.
Louis:	Miss a turn.
All:	Move it forward, move it back, miss a turn.
	Forward, back, forward . . .
Drum:	It's done.
Dorene:	I won.
Louis:	Now, let's just be silly,
Drum:	and make too much noise,
All:	and laugh a lot,
Drum and Dorene:	because we have a new friend,
Louis:	because I have two new friends.
Dorene:	Let's just be willy-nilly silly,
All:	and laugh. Because we want to.

Tall Tale, Too

Drum:	Once, I saw a dog that was ninety feet long.
Dorene and Louis:	**You did?**
Drum:	I did. And this dog was always trying to hide, so he could jump out and surprise people.
Dorene and Louis:	**He hid?**
Drum:	He tried to. He tried to squeeze his big self under rosebushes and up against tree trunks. But the people were never surprised.
Dorene:	Not surprised, no. So . . .
Drum:	So then, he found out that if he turned himself around and around, and tied himself up with his tail, he looked just like a package.
Louis:	And then . . .

Drum:	And then, some people came along and found him, and they put him under their . . .
Dorene:	Christmas tree!
Drum:	Uh-huh, and early Christmas morning, they unwrapped him, and he jumped up and said . . .
Dorene and Louis:	**"Surprise!"**
Drum:	Yeah. And with his big old, ninety-foot-long self, he bent the whole house out of shape, until the house looked just like him. So the people built a new house that was . . .
Dorene:	ninety-*one* feet long!
Drum:	Yeah. And then . . .
All:	**And then, they all lived happily ever after. Yeah!**

Going to Get Rae

Dorene: On the plane with Grandma,

I'm thinking about my cousin, Rae.

Is she feeling sad right now,

knowing we'll be taking her away?

If I had to leave my mother,

I would cry a thousand tears.

Every day away from her

would be a thousand years.

I want to help my cousin,

so I'll sit real still, and then,

I'll close my eyes and pray her mom

will soon be well again.

F O U R

Drum, Dorene, Louis and Rae

Rae

Rae: I'm not going to put my clothes away.

I won't be here long,

just until Mama's a little bit

stronger, then the faster I finish

packing, the faster I'll get home.

Then, I'll be able to help Mama walk.

I can be her arm, too,

and when she tries to talk,

I'll listen extra hard.

I'm keeping my clothes in the suitcase.

I'm not going to be here long.

Promise

Dorene: Come on, Rae,
  let's go outside.
  Come and meet
  my friends.
  I promise that
  we'll make you smile,
  before this evening
  ends.

24

Playground

All:	We're running,
Dorene:	we're sliding,
Louis:	swinging,
Rae:	sweating.
All:	Water drips from our faces.
Drum:	Our backs are wet.
Louis:	Get out the bottles of water.
All:	Find some shade.
Rae:	Sit.
Dorene:	Drink.
Louis:	Flop.
Drum:	Rest.
All:	*Ahhhhh.*

The Friendly Four

Drum:	Didn't I call this summer a bummer?
All:	Not anymore, not anymore.
Drum:	I was alone, and life was lonely.
All:	But not anymore,
Drum:	'cause we're the Friendly Four!
Louis, Dorene, Rae:	The Friendly Four?
Drum:	The Friendly Four.
All:	We'll call ourselves the Friendly Four.
Drum:	Bummer's gone and lonely, too,
Louis:	We showed them what good friends can do,
Rae:	We sent them flying out the door,
All:	'Cause we're all here, and we're the Friendly Four.

Rain

Dorene:	I've got the ball. Catch.
Louis:	I think it's going to rain.
Rae:	I don't want it to rain.
Drum and Dorene:	Neither do I.
Louis:	But the sky looks funny.
Drum, Dorene, Rae:	It's not going to rain.
Louis:	The air smells funny.
Drum, Dorene, Rae:	It's not going to rain.
Louis:	The wind is doing funny things.
Drum, Dorene, Rae:	It's not going to . . .
All:	Rain! Run!

The Fuss

Dorene and Rae: One day we had a mighty fuss,

every single one of us.

All: We were kicking the ball, and everything

was fine,

until the ball went over the line.

Drum and Louis: Then one of us said, "That's not fair!"

Dorene and Rae: Another one said, "I don't care!"

Drum: Then we were all yelling.

Rae: Our jaws were swelling.

Louis: Tears were welling up in our eyes.

Dorene and Rae: We went home mad, with nobody talking,

the only sound was . . .

All: . . . eight feet walking.

Drum and Louis: But the very next day, we were all

All: outside again, kicking that ball.

Punished

All: I'm looking out my window,

wishing I hadn't done it.

I could be with my friends, right now,

having fun.

It's not as if we didn't know.

We went where we weren't

supposed to go.

The grown-ups had told us not to travel

beyond the corner tree.

When they looked, they couldn't find us,

now we're punished to remind us

not to forget to remember

where we're supposed to be.

When Summer Ends

Rae: Today I had a surprise. The phone

rang, and it was Mama.

I could understand every word

she said. She told me how much

she misses me. I miss her more.

She said I can come home

when summer is over.

I'll be so happy when I can

touch her face, and she can touch

mine.

The only thing is,

I wish my friends could go with me.

I'll be glad, and sorry, too,

when summer ends.

Let's Make a Town

Louis: Let's make a town.

Drum, Dorene, Rae: Where will we make it?

Louis: In Drum's yard, with cardboard and paint.

Rae: We'll make a good town, a good summer town.

Dorene: We'll call it the town of Goodsummer.

All: Let's make a town, a good summer town.

                                  We'll call it the town of Goodsummer, Goodsummer,

                                  we'll call it the town of Goodsummer.

Here Comes the Truck

All: Here comes the truck,

                carrying sheets of cardboard,

                cans of paint, and brushes,

Drum and Rae: carrying sticky tape,

                and colored paper,

                and markers,

Dorene and Louis: and glitter

                and glue.

All: Now we have everything

                we need, to make a town

                that has beauty and laughter

                and heart.

Louis: Let's get started!

We Did It!

Rae: We painted for days and days,

Louis: Monday through Friday,

                      and Monday through Friday again

Louis and Rae: (not counting the day Drum knocked over

                      a can of paint, and we had to clean it up).

Dorene: But now, it's finished,

                      so let's lift our tired arms and say,

All: "Hooray! We did it! We built our own town!"

Drum: We've got:

All: One bank, one library, one church,

                      two toy stores, one bookstore, one school,

                      and so forth, and so forth.

Rae: To get here, just drive

                      south, east, west and north.

Drum: You can't miss it. Look for

                      the sign that says:

All: Welcome to the Town of Goodsummer

                      Population   4

One Week Later
FIVE

In the Town of Goodsummer

Parade

All: We'll get the paintings from the garage,

and stand them around the fence.

Today, we're going to celebrate.

Drum: Welcome, ladies and gents!

All: Thank you for coming to our parade,

and now, without a pause,

we'll march by in our grown-up clothes.

Dorene: Thank you for your applause.

All: We turned the music way up loud,

to show you that we're happy and proud

of the work we did to build our town.

Now, watch us as we march around,

and around, and around, and around.

Mmmarch! Mmmarch!

Mmmarch! March! MARCH!

At the Movies

Drum:	Is the monster still on the screen?
Rae:	Yes. He's stomping.
	I'm looking with one eye closed.
Louis:	I'm looking the other way.
Drum:	I'm covering my face.
Dorene:	My head is in my lap. What's he doing now?
Rae:	He's waving his fist.
Drum, Dorene, Louis:	Ohhhh!
Louis:	What's he doing now?
Rae:	He's running . . .
Drum, Dorene, Louis:	Oh no! He's running!
Rae:	. . . away. The people are chasing *him*.
All:	Yaaay!
Rae:	That was a great movie.
	That monster was mean!
Drum, Dorene, Louis:	That was the best movie I have ever not seen.

38

At the Bank

Louis:　May I help you, ma'am?

Rae:　Yes, you may. I want to hear what

you have to say.

Tell me, please, the exact amount

of money I have in my bank account.

Louis:　Well, I won't keep you in suspense,

you have one million dollars and fifty cents.

Now have a good day, and come back soon.

Rae:　I'll come back tomorrow at noon,

with another million and quarters (two),

so until tomorrow, I say goodbye

to you.

Louis:　May I help you, sir?

Drum:　Yes, you may. I want to hear what

you have to say.

Dorene:　I'm the clock. *Dong! Dong! Dong!*

So long, the bank is closed for the day.

At School

All: You want five hours of recess,

and fifteen minutes of work?

Yes, my students, yes, indeed,

you're wise to want to shirk.

You want an ounce or two

of homework,

and ten tons of TV?

Yes, my students, yes, indeed,

I certainly agree.

I see you're laughing, now, and so,

I guess I'll have to smile.

You were only teasing? Well, I

knew it all the while.

At the Office Building

Dorene:	I'm calling you on the phone.
Drum:	I'm not here, I'm at a meeting.
	Leave a message after the beep.
Dorene:	I'm calling you on the phone.
Rae:	I'm not here, I'm out of town.
	Leave a message after the beep.
Dorene:	I'm calling you on the phone.
Louis:	I'm not here, I'm making a speech.
	Leave a message after the beep.
Drum, Louis, Rae:	I'm calling you on the phone.
Dorene:	Leave a message after the beep.
	I got tired of calling and went home.
	I'm fast asleep.

At the Library

Rae:	Good morning.
Drum, Dorene, Louis:	Good morning. I'd like a book about
Dorene:	a bubbly brook.
Drum:	a pastry cook.
Louis:	a pinto horse.
Rae:	Of course. Here's one for you,
	one for you, and one for you.

Drum, Dorene, Louis:	I'm back, and this time,
	I'd like a book about
Dorene:	how to swim without water.
Drum:	how to make a cloud rain lemonade.
Louis:	how to teach a spider to speak.
Rae:	Sorry, those books are not on the shelves.
	Try again next week.

At the Pet Shop

All: What a shop!

          The animals live in luxury,

Louis: in their own large rooms,

Dorene: with big beds, and soft chairs,

All: and mirrors.

Drum: When somebody comes to buy them,

          they say,

All: "No! I don't want to go!"

Rae: Where else will they have silk bathrobes

Louis: and sandals,

All: to show off, when people come to visit?

At the Concert Hall

All:	We look wonderful
Dorene and Rae:	in our gowns and gloves, hats,
Drum and Louis:	tuxedos,
All:	going to the concert.
	Now, we're there, listening to
Drum:	the horns,
Rae:	the strings,
Louis:	the piano,
Dorene:	the drums,
All:	all playing together,
Drum:	making music that thunders,
Rae:	music that swings,
Louis:	lullabies, waltzes,
Dorene:	hymns.
All:	And now, to the banquet hall for dinner.
	We take the music with us,
	tingling on our skin, playing again
	in our heads and in our hearts.

SIX
Goodbyes

Goodbye, Rae

Louis: Drum and I are sad to see Rae go.
On the way home from the airport,
we see a plane in the sky,
and we pretend it's hers.

Drum: We wave until it's out of sight.
Tomorrow night, Dorene and her
grandma will be back,

Drum and Louis: but school will be starting soon.

Our summer vacation is over.

E-mail

Dear Friendly Four Family:

I really, really, really, really

miss you.

(My mother is helping me spell.)

I don't have much to tell you,

except that Mama is almost like she

used to be. She wants to meet you

(Drum and Louis)

so we're both coming to visit

next summer.

                Love,

                Rae

P. S. I really meant all those reallys!

        Didn't we have fun?

GOOD

Goodbye to Goodsummer

Drum: The summer started out with one,

Dorene: and now there are four, and even though

one of us is far away,

Drum, Dorene, Louis: we're still together.

We'll find some fall, winter

and spring things to laugh about,

Louis: and our town will wait for us.

Drum, Dorene, Louis: So, goodbye for now, Goodsummer.

We'll see you next year.

47

*For the wonderful boys of the "Five Thousand Role Models"
program, Miami-Dade County, Florida, elementary schools,
and for all the many young people who have the courage
to make good lives for themselves and create a path
for others to follow*
–E.G.

To my dear friend Helen Burleson, for your love of children
–J.S.G.